Economically Developing Cou~~ntries~~

Vietna~~m~~

Ole Steen Hansen

HODDER
Wayland

an imprint of Hodder Children's Books

Economically Developing Countries

Brazil   **India**

China   **Malaysia**

Egypt   **Vietnam**

Cover: A mobile restaurant in Ho Chi Minh City, being carried to its roadside location.

Title page: Names in Vietnam have meanings. This woman is called Nguyet, which means moon. This type of hat is worn by most women in Vietnam.

Contents page: Rush hour in bustling Ho Chi Minh City.

Picture acknowledgements: All photographs including the cover are by Ole Steen Hansen, except for: Eye Ubiquitous (Tim Page) 18 (inset), 19; Topham 15. All artwork was provided by Peter Bull.

Editor: Polly Goodman
Designer: Mark Whitchurch

First published in 1996 by Wayland Publishers Ltd.
This edition updated and reprinted in 2001 by Hodder Wayland,
an imprint of Hodder Children's Books.

British Library Cataloguing in Publication Data
Hansen Ole Steen
    Vietnam. - (Economically Developing
    Countries Series)
    I. Title II. Series
    916.2

ISBN 0 7502 3480 6

Printed and bound by G. Canale & C.S.pA., Turin, Italy

Hodder Children's Books
A Division of Hodder Headline Limited
338 Euston Road, London NW1 3BH

Contents

'It's better now'

The words, 'It's better now' are often heard in Vietnam, when people compare their present situation with the past. For half of the last 2,000 years Vietnam has been occupied by foreign powers. Many people associate Vietnam with the American war, when the US government sent troops into Vietnam in the 1960s, to support the South Vietnamese government in their conflict with local guerrillas and communist North Vietnam. But during the last 100 years, three of the world's greatest powers – France, Japan and the USA – have in turn conquered, occupied, or dominated all or parts of Vietnam. It has been subjected to devastation on a scale seldom – if ever – equalled in world history. Yet time and again the Vietnamese have repelled their powerful enemies.

The revolutionary colours are held high for the twentieth anniversary of the capture of Saigon in 1975. Politically, Vietnam is a communist country, but the economy is adopting capitalism at breakneck speed.

4

Shopping in Cholon, the Chinese part of Ho Chi Minh City, Vietnam. A new optimism is felt in most areas of this once war-torn country.

The ravages of war have left Vietnam among the poorest nations on earth. On top of this, from 1979 to 1992 Vietnam was economically isolated. Except for help from communist countries, international aid was cut off entirely. Vietnam had to stand on its own feet to rebuild itself. However, even after the economic crisis in Southeast Asia from 1996–1997, the Vietnamese economy is recovering. The average economic growth rate from 1990–98 was an impressive 6.1 per cent and people's standard of living is getting better.

The road ahead is scattered with obstacles, and Vietnam will not become rich overnight. But most people hold the optimistic view that 'It's better now' – and the future could be even better!

'My family fled from Vietnam when I was very small. At 21 years old I went back to study art in Hanoi. At first I thought, "What are you doing here in the noise, the heat and dust?" Everything was so different from Canada where I grew up. But now as I'm going home after ten months I know I'll miss Vietnam badly. The people are so friendly here. It's not a bad feeling knowing I was born in Hanoi.'
*– **Mai Phan, a Vietnamese-Canadian (left)***

The natural environment

Vietnam is a strikingly beautiful country of rivers, paddy fields, plains and wild, inaccessible mountains. It is 1,600 km long and its shape on the map resembles a sea-horse heading out into the South China Sea. The distance between North and South Vietnam is the same as the distance between New York and Florida. Vietnam's land area is slightly larger than Italy's, though it is 400 km longer from north to south, and is only 50 km wide at the narrowest point.

VIETNAM AT A GLANCE	
Capital city	Hanoi
Important cities	Ho Chi Minh City (Saigon up to 1975), Haiphong, Hue, Danang, Can Tho, Vinh
Land area	331,041 square kilometres
Highest mountain	Fan Si Phan: 3,143 metres
Length of coastline	3,260 kilometres (more if islands are included)

Right *Vietnam's main geographical features. The sources of the two biggest rivers – the Mekong and the Red River – are found in China.*

CHINA

Fan Si Pan, 3,143 metres

Northern Mountains

Dién Bién

Red River

Hanoi

Hai Phong

RED RIVER DELTA

N

Vinh

SOUTH CHINA SEA

LAOS

Quang Tri

Huê

Da Nang

Hôi An

Troung Son Mountains

CAMBODIA

Nha Trang

Above *A Vietnamese fish market.*

Biên Hoa

Hô Chi Minh

My Tho

Vung Tau

Cân Tho

Mekong

MEKONG DELTA

| 0 | 100 | 200 | 300 km |
| 0 | 100 | | 200 miles |

Paddy fields among the North-west Mountains, close to the Laos border.

Three-quarters of Vietnam's landscape consists of mountains and plateaus. The Troung Son Mountains along the Cambodian and Laos borders are the spine of the country. Many small rivers have their source here, and wind their way across the narrow coastal plains out to the sea. The sources of the two biggest rivers – the Mekong and the Red River – are found much further north, in China. Both rivers carry large amount of silt and have created two important deltas at either end of the country. These deltas grow larger each year.

VIETNAM'S FIVE LANDSCAPES

The *Red River Delta* is the cradle of Vietnamese culture and one of the world's most densely populated areas. The country's most important agricultural area is the *Mekong Delta*. The shape of Vietnam is often said to look like a long bamboo pole with a rice basket at each end. This is a good comparison, since the two deltas are indeed the rice baskets of the country. The *Northern Mountains* are where most of the country's mineral resources, such as coal and metals are found. During the American war, the *Central Highlands* were infamous for much heavy fighting. However, they are now an area for development and resettlement of people from crowded parts of the country. The *Coastal Plains* are the narrow strip of land down the length of the country.

7

VIETNAM'S FORESTS

Forest covers 25 per cent of Vietnam. Some parts are very old, and due to their inaccessibility, they have been left untouched by human activity. Unfortunately, other parts have been totally destroyed. US forces defoliated 1.7 million hectares (71 per cent of the UK's total area of forest) during the American war, to help soldiers spot their enemies in the jungle. But the largest areas have been cut down by the Vietnamese themselves, to cater for a growing demand for construction timber, firewood and timber for the export market.

DEFORESTATION IN VIETNAM	
Percentage of original forest	
1998	44%
1996	29%
1995	20%
Source: *Lonely Planet, 1999*	

Deforestation threatens to wipe out rare species of plants and animals. It also leads to soil erosion in the highlands, which makes the rivers more difficult to control, resulting in higher risk of flooding in the deltas. The government runs several projects to preserve and reestablish the forests of Vietnam. National Parks like the Cuc Phuong National Park, 140 km south of Hanoi, have been established. However, money is in short supply, and at the moment it pays better to exploit the forests.

'We estimate Vietnam has more than 12,000 species of plants, though only about 7,000 have been identified. More than 2,000, like this one [in the photo, left]*, can be used for food, medicine and wood products.'* – **Do Cuong, from Cuc Phuong National Park**

In North Vietnam, the end of winter brings months of drizzling rain, which makes the air very humid.

CLIMATE IN VIETNAM

Key: 1 = Average temperature in °C
     2 = Rain in mm
     3 = Daily hours of sunshine (hrs:mins)

	Ho Chi Minh City			Hanoi		
	1	2	3	1	2	3
Jan	25	16	6:38	15	22	1:24
Feb	26	3	7:40	17	36	1:24
March	27	13	7:24	19	45	1:18
April	28	42	6:34	23	89	2.12
May	28	220	4:39	27	216	4:12
June	27	331	3:54	29	254	5:00
July	26	314	3:12	28	335	4:48
Aug	27	269	3:51	28	339	4:12
Sept	26	336	3:16	27	276	4:18
Oct	26	269	4:05	24	115	4:12
Nov	26	115	4:56	21	48	3:12
Dec	26	56	5:27	18	27	2:06

CLIMATE

North Vietnam has a more extreme climate than the rest of the country: snow can fall in the mountains. Even in the southern Red River Delta, the temperature may drop to around 8 °C in winter. Most houses have no heating, so this can feel very cold indeed. The end of winter brings several months of seemingly never-ending drizzling rain (called 'rain dust' in Vietnamese), which makes the air very humid and drying the washing next to impossible. The northern summer brings extremely hot weather and sometimes violent, devastating typhoons.

In contrast the climate in the south is tropical. The weather is hot all year round – though not as hot as the summer in the north. Evenings can be very pleasant, with temperatures around 26 °C, and no burning sun. The south has a rainy and a dry season, but even during the rainy season the rain doesn't fall continuously.

Although the average rainfall in Vietnam is sufficient, parts of the country are sometimes hit by drought. In 1994, 50,000 people in the Central Highlands were starving because drought had destroyed their crops.

Hard-won independence

Like some other Southeast Asian peoples, the Vietnamese emigrated from southern China in prehistoric times. They settled in the fertile Red River Delta area. This land was conquered by the Chinese in 111 BC and remained under Chinese rule for more than 1,000 years. Chinese rule was often harsh, but also introduced the Vietnamese to rice growing, the metal plough, Chinese religions and educational systems. Many Chinese beliefs and traditions became part of everyday life and have remained so to this day. The fierce will to fight for national independence also became part of Vietnam's heritage during those years, and in the end the Chinese were forced out.

TIME LINE

111 BC – 938 AD CHINESE OCCUPATION OF VIETNAM.

1656 THE KINGDOM OF CHAMPA IS DESTROYED BY THE VIETNAMESE.

1802 THE COUNTRY COVERS THE AREA KNOWN AS VIETNAM TODAY.

1858 THE FRENCH START COLONIZING VIETNAM.

1887 ALL VIETNAM BECOMES A FRENCH COLONY.

1940 THE JAPANESE INVADE VIETNAM IN THE SECOND WORLD WAR.

1945 HO CHI MINH DECLARES VIETNAM'S INDEPENDENCE, BUT THE FRENCH RETURN TO RECLAIM THEIR COLONY.

1954 THE FRENCH ARE DEFEATED AT DIEN BIEN PHU. VIETNAM IS DIVIDED ALONG THE SEVENTEENTH PARALLEL.

1964 USA STARTS BOMBING NORTH VIETNAM.

1965 FIRST US MARINES LAND AT DANANG.

1975 USA EVACUATES ITS LAST REPRESENTATIVES FROM SAIGON. VIETNAM IS REUNIFIED UNDER NORTHERN COMMUNIST RULE.

1978 VIETNAM INVADES CAMBODIA.

1979 CHINA ATTACKS NORTHERN PROVINCES OF VIETNAM.

1986 DOI MOI IS INTRODUCED AFTER LACK OF SUCCESS IN THE SOCIALIST ECONOMY.

1994 USA LIFTS ECONOMIC EMBARGO.

1995 VIETNAM BECOMES A MEMBER OF THE SOUTHEAST ASIAN NATIONS (ASEAN).

1996–97 ECONOMIC CRISIS IN SOUTHEAST ASIA

A statue of the Goddess of Mercy, the most popular divinity to both the Chinese and Vietnamese cultures.

10

According to ancient Vietnamese/Chinese tradition the dead continue to live in some kind of underworld. Here they need all sort of things for their daily life – houses, servants, money, cars, clothes, radios… you name it! It is the duty of the living to provide these things. In practice everything is constructed out of paper, and pretend money is printed. Until recently only the local currency was made, but as a sign of the changing times in Vietnam, US dollars are becoming increasingly popular with the dead! Everything is transferred to the other world by being burned at either the ancestor's altar at home or at the local pagoda. Not all modern Vietnamese believe their dead ancestors live on and actually receive the gifts. But most keep these traditions alive as a way of paying respect.

A funeral at the Tran Quoc Pagoda in Hanoi. Paper offerings to be burnt for the dead include a gas burner for the kitchen, a fan to keep cool, money, a ghetto blaster, clothes, hats and shoes.

Vietnam then expanded southwards in a process that ended only about 200 years ago. The kingdom of Champa in present day central Vietnam was the first area to be conquered. Later, the lower Mekong Delta, which had been part of Cambodia, was taken. The French took over this much-larger Vietnam as a colony during the nineteenth century.

The Temple of Literature university, which was founded in 1070, 422 years before Columbus first visited America.

11

FRENCH YEARS

In 1887 France claimed all Vietnam to be part of its Indochinese Union, which also included Cambodia and Laos. From 1940-45 Vietnam was occupied by Japan. Apart from this period, France ruled the country until 1954, when its army was defeated by Vietnamese liberation forces in the battle of Dien Bien Phu.

Vietnam changed dramatically under French rule. The Vietnamese were ruthlessly exploited. The French built the Saigon – Hanoi railroad, better ports and irrigation systems. But these were paid for by heavily taxed peasants, and profits from the lucrative opium, alcohol and salt monopolies. They also introduced a new system of script, based on the European alphabet. This turned out to be a blessing, since the new Vietnamese alphabet was much easier to learn than the Chinese characters that had been used before. The French left Vietnam with a larger Catholic population than any other Southeast Asian country, except for the Philippines. Caodaism, a Vietnamese religion

Inside the Cao Dai temple at Tay Ninh. According to Caodaism, the divine truth is communicated through spirits. Mediums have allegedly been in contact with deceased famous people of both East and West – among them Shakespeare, Joan of Arc, Victor Hugo and Lenin.

UNCLE HO

Ho Chi Minh was born in 1890. After spending 30 years in various countries, he came to see communism as the way forward for oppressed peoples in the colonies. Under his leadership the French were forced to leave Vietnam. Later he led North Vietnam in the American war. Ho Chi Minh became a worldwide symbol of the courageous Vietnamese stand against the world's greatest military power. Although a communist, Ho Chi Minh was foremost a nationalist who wanted independence for his people. His private life-style was as simple and spartan as that of most Vietnamese. He became deeply respected all over Vietnam and was affectionately known as Uncle Ho. He died in 1969.

__Right__ Ho Chi Minh's portrait on a 5,000 Dong note.

developed in these years, is a mixture of old Chinese/Vietnamese religions, Islam, Christianity, Hinduism and a belief in the spirit world.

Few Vietnamese benefited from colonial rule. Most were left poorer, landless and determined to continue their country's tradition of expelling foreign invaders.

__Above__ Incense is burned to honour Ho Chi Minh at this memorial site erected in his native village.

__Left__ The bakery is a hot place to work in the tropics. Bread is a legacy of French rule, and is still widely popular in Vietnam.

THE AMERICAN WAR

Vietnam was divided into North and South Vietnam after the French left in 1954. The North was under communist rule. Back in 1945, Ho Chi Minh had hoped for American support against the French. The US government decided not to help, so Ho Chi Minh turned to communist Russia for support.

South Vietnam was ruled by various corrupt anti-communist rulers, who had little support from their own people. Eventually, protests against the South Vietnamese government turned into civil war. The southern government forces were losing from the start. The rebel Vietcong guerrillas had support from the north, and soon controlled large areas of the countryside. The US, fearing that Vietnam would become entirely communist, decided to give military support to the South Vietnamese government.

A US heavy gun at the War Crimes Exhibition in Ho Chi Minh City. The US forces used many heavy weapons to try to defeat their enemy.

The US government believed their superior firepower and technology would do what the southern government, and the French, had failed to – beat the Vietnamese guerrillas. US planes dropped more bombs in Vietnam than had been used in Europe during the whole of the Second World War. Paddy fields and forests were sprayed with poisonous defoliant to deny the guerrillas food and cover. Thousands of helicopters searched for and tried to destroy the guerrillas. Frequently though, it was still very difficult to find them. Often US soldiers found themselves in well-prepared ambushes. It was a confused war, with no front lines. The US government did not invade North Vietnam for fear of communist Russia or China joining in the war. But they tried to force the north to stop their support of the guerrillas in the south by means of massive air raids.

A weeping Vietnamese woman looks on with a government soldier, as flames consume her village in the American war.

The Americans claimed a great many times that they were just about to win the war. However, during the lunar new year festival of Tet in 1968, the communist guerrillas launched attacks in many large cities in South Vietnam. The US military base at Khe Sanh was under siege for 77 days. After the initial shock, the US government hit back hard. The communist forces suffered a severe military defeat. Yet because of the Tet offensive, the war became more unpopular than ever in the US, and opinion around the world swung against it. The US forces had won the battle, but politically speaking they were losing, because few people

A North Vietnamese teenager at war

Bang had a typical Vietnamese childhood in a coastal village near Hai Phong. She spent her days riding out to the paddy fields on the buffalo in the early morning, catching fish and crabs in the canals and paddy fields, swimming, going to school in the afternoon and spending time with her family in the evening. But her teenage years were very different. From 1964 American jets would frequently fly over the village. Bang can remember being frightened at first, but she soon came to accept the sight of planes screaming low overhead to avoid the anti-aircraft guns. The village men were called up for service and sent south. Bang's brothers and her brother-in-law went, too. Her brother-in-law was later killed crossing a river in the Mekong Delta. The boys from her class also

Bang at 16 years old. Her elder brother served as a mortarman in the army. He carried this picture as a good luck charm in the Khe Sanh battle and through four more years of fighting, and survived.

went. The sounds of mourning became a common occurrence in the village as yet another household received a letter telling them a relative had been killed in the war.

For a time Bang had to leave school to help her hard-pressed parents in the fields. Desperate to study, she managed to read classic novels whilst handling the buffalo. Teachers were believed they could or should win. Slowly, the US government began to withdraw its forces, leaving a disillusioned south Vietnamese army to handle its own affairs. In 1975, the north Vietnamese launched a large-scale attack on the south. Although the south Vietnamese army was the largest, it collapsed. In a few months the south was 'liberated'. Not everyone in the south saw the situation as a liberation, but for the first time in many years, the country was unified under Vietnamese leadership. Ho Chi Minh's dream had finally come true, although he didn't live long enough to see it, as he died in 1969.

Below Bang, just outside her childhood home by a bridge in the village.

'The war broke my teenage dreams of studying and travelling. They were very hard years and sometimes I wonder how I managed at all. But everybody in the village shared a common feeling of determination. We all wanted to do our duty. We wanted to serve our country. Personal comfort and safety came second. I hope it will never happen again though.'
– Vu Thuy Bang, Hai Phong

in short supply, so after some years Bang – against her wishes – found herself teaching. She volunteered to teach in liberated areas in the south. This was a dangerous job, since these areas were still attacked by US forces. The army told her to stay at home. Her brothers were already in the army, and someone had to survive to look after her elderly parents.

Today Bang lives peacefully with her friendly family in a small house in Hai Phong.

Below Bang outside her house today, preparing meat for a family lunch of crispy Vietnamese spring rolls.

Main Picture This man is making artificial limbs in a centre at Can Tho. Vietnam's wars have ensured him full employment for many years to come.

Inset This small sign is the only warning of a minefield, a leftover from the war with Cambodia.

INVASION OF CAMBODIA

Peace lasted only for a few years. In Cambodia the Khmer Rouge took over the government. They killed one million of Cambodia's 7 million people and made repeated border attacks against Vietnam. These attacks were stopped in 1978, when the Vietnamese invaded Cambodia. Mines were used extensively in this war, and many people were crippled by them. Often, younger Vietnamese remember this as 'the war', rather than the war with the USA. China, which sided with the Khmer Rouge, decided to teach Vietnam a lesson and attacked Vietnam's northern provinces. Much destruction was caused, but China's army was badly mauled by the battle-hardened Vietnamese.

Most countries in the world – headed by the US – saw the invasion of Cambodia as an act of Vietnamese aggression, and imposed a trade embargo on Vietnam. As a result, the country was left isolated and devastated after decades of war.

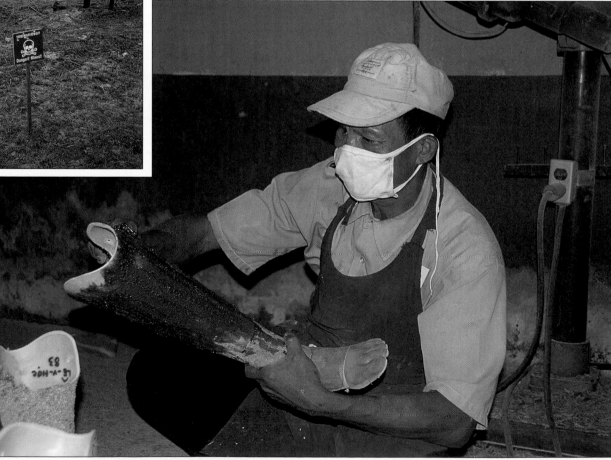

THE ROAD TO DOI MOI

The communists from the north tried to turn the economy in the south to socialism. In the process, many people had their property confiscated and were politically repressed. This policy led to huge numbers leaving the country as refugees. The 'boat people' made headlines all over the world. However, the new socialist economy didn't come up with any spectacular results. Living conditions got worse, inflation soared, and the trade embargo meant that Vietnam received little international help to rebuild the country. To improve the situation the government introduced Doi Moi, an economic policy allowing some free enterprise. Vietnam left Cambodia in 1989 and has now successfully attracted foreign investors. The communist government still allows no political opposition, but the economy is developing fast. A great many refugees are coming back and Vietnam is now returning to the arena of world affairs.

Many ethnic Chinese left Vietnam after the communists took over the south. This ethnic Chinese man is being held in a refugee camp in Hong Kong.

The people

Inhabitants per Km²

Over 5000	150-250
1000-5000	50-150
500-1000	20-50
250-500	Under 20

POPULATION DENSITY

(Inhabitants per square kilometre)

Bangladesh	873
Japan	336
UK	242
Vietnam	240
Malaysia	68
USA	29
Australia	2

Source: *Population Reference Bureau, 1999*

With a population of almost 80 million people (2000), Vietnam has the twelfth-largest population in the world. It has more than doubled since 1960 and is expected to reach over 108 million by the year 2025. The large population is both an advantage and a hindrance to the much-needed development of the country.

The Vietnamese have a reputation for being well educated and hardworking. Thus many people see the population itself as being Vietnam's biggest asset. As the Vietnamese become more wealthy, the sheer number of people means that Vietnam could become a highly attractive market for companies wanting to sell goods and services. In addition, foreign companies wanting to invest in Vietnam will be able to find efficient employees for their businesses.

On the other hand, the population is big enough already. Population density in the delta areas is very high. In large agricultural areas around Hanoi the density is about 1,000 inhabitants per square kilometre. This density is higher than the average density of Bangladesh, which is the most densely populated country in the world.

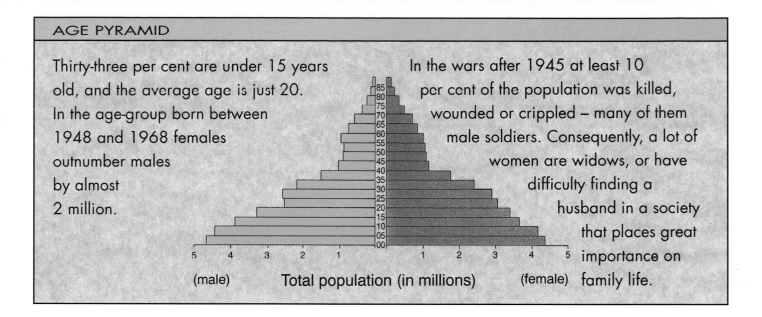

AGE PYRAMID

Thirty-three per cent are under 15 years old, and the average age is just 20. In the age-group born between 1948 and 1968 females outnumber males by almost 2 million.

In the wars after 1945 at least 10 per cent of the population was killed, wounded or crippled – many of them male soldiers. Consequently, a lot of women are widows, or have difficulty finding a husband in a society that places great importance on family life.

85 80 75 70 65 60 55 50 45 40 35 30 25 20 15 10 05 00

5 4 3 2 1   1 2 3 4 5

(male)   Total population (in millions)   (female)

The big cities of Hanoi, Ho Chi Minh City and Haiphong are crowded, too. The population density of Ho Chi Minh City is comparable to the density that would result from the entire English population being squeezed inside the M25 motorway around London.

Space isn't the only problem. Finding a job is already very difficult. But each year 1.2 million school leavers join the work-force, while only 200,000 people leave it. The government sees birth control as essential and has more than doubled its budget for family planning. The birth control programme has been quite successful in the cities, but less so in the villages. The government is also trying to encourage people to resettle in the less-populated Central Highlands.

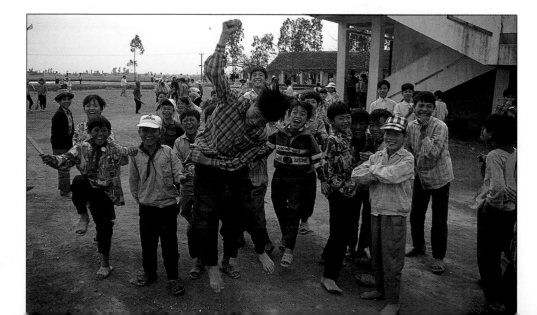

Village schoolboys in the Red River Delta area. Eighty per cent of Vietnamese people live in rural areas.

Tourism and tradition in a border village

Ha Cong Guong is 58 years old and belongs to the white Thai minority. His language is very similar to the language spoken in Thailand, but of course he speaks fluent Vietnamese as well. Ha Cong Guong has been living in villages close to the Laos border all his life and has seldom been away from the area. When he was a child, wild tigers would sometimes be seen in the village. Life has always been traditional, but it is now changing rapidly. Cooking is still done over open fires in the kitchen inside the 90-year-old stilted wooden house. But Guong's wife now has the option of listening to the ghetto blaster while working. This and other modern luxuries (television, refrigerators, French wines) are the result of increasing numbers of tourists visiting the village. They like to see the old Thai culture, and this has been turned into good business. For example, traditional weavings, made by the women are sold to visitors. The family members expect to live in the village for the rest of their lives, but they hope that their grand-daughter will go to Hanoi university to study.

Above *Ha Cong Guong's daughter-in-law weaving in the house.* **Inset** *Traditional weavings like this are popular souvenirs with the tourists.*

'We like to invite tourists into our home. They can stay a few days, buy crafts or just have a look around. We are happy about the government's new policies. Many mountain villages are poor. Our contact with tourists makes it possible to raise our standard of living.' – **Ha Cong Guong, Mai Chau village in the North-west Mountains (left)**

FAMILY LIFE

The family is the central social unit of life in Vietnam. It is considered very important to belong to a family, to visit relatives, to help and support them. Social security is provided by the family rather than the state, and there is nothing unusual in three generations living together in one house.

An average Vietnamese family gets up at about five in the morning. Everyone sits together on mats on the floor for a breakfast of noodle soup, rice or bread. If the family members get up late, the children may have their breakfast at one of the little street stalls on the way to school. The whole family will return home for a lunch of rice, soup, meat or vegetables. A break in the heat of midday is common all over Vietnam. In the afternoon the parents go back to work, while the children can look forward to three hours of home studies. Most homes have no fridge, so shopping at the market is a daily activity. Food will not stay fresh for long in the hot climate. The evening meal is usually similar to lunch.

A Vietnamese family sitting together on the family vehicle. In the background you can see their house.

'I have 6 sisters and one brother. My parents had to try and try and try again before they got the son they wanted. Today I have my own family, lots of relatives and friends. When I went away to study, 30 family members came with me to the railway station on 7 motorbikes – they all wanted to wish me a safe journey. I am very lucky.' – **Vo Thi Sinh, Vinh City**

Traditionally, the man is the head of the family, and many Vietnamese men help with the cooking. Grandparents also help around the house. After supper there is time for playing, watching television or visiting friends before it's time to go to bed. Traditional Vietnamese beds consist of woven straw matting on top of wooden planks, and are covered with mosquito nets.

Above *Vo Thi Sinh making tea. Traditionally, guests are always welcomed into a Vietnamese home by being served tea.*

The family eats in a big circle, sitting on mats laid out on the floor.

MINORITIES

The ethnic Vietnamese make up 87 per cent of the country's population and are mostly found in the delta areas and coastal provinces. But no less than 54 ethnic minorities also live in Vietnam. Some were living in the area even before the Vietnamese settled there in prehistoric times. Most ethnic minorities live in the less crowded mountain areas. In the far North-west Mountains the Vietnamese make up less than 20 per cent of the population. Ethnic minorities in the highlands are often known as *montagnards* – the French word for highlanders.

One ethnic minority is distinctly different from the rest. Whereas most minorities often live in remote areas, the Chinese are right in the mainstream of the modern developments. Half of Vietnam's Chinese population lives in Cholon, the Chinatown of Ho Chi Minh City. Traditionally, the Chinese have always been involved in trade and business, and have been mistrusted by the communist government since 1975. Around 1979 the situation got so bad that many Chinese decided to leave Vietnam. Many of the boat people were ethnic Chinese. The situation is better now, and the Chinese are back in business.

IMPORTANT ETHNIC MINORITIES IN VIETNAM			
Minority group	**Location**	**Population in millions**	**Percentage of population**
Mon-Khmer	Mekong Delta/Cambodian border/ Central Vietnam	1.7	2.6 %
Austronesians	Central south Vietnam/Cambodian border	0.6	1 %
Tay-Thai	North-west Mountains	3	4.8 %
Hmong Dao	North-west Mountains	0.9	1.4 %
Tibetan-Burmese	North-west Mountains	0.29	0.04 %
Chinese	Ho Chi Minh City/Mekong Delta/ southern coast/north-east Vietnam	1	1.5 %

Feeding the people

Vietnam is now the second-largest exporter of rice in the world, but still not everyone has enough to eat. During the winter of 1993–94 ethnic minorities living around Quang Tri suffered the worst food shortage in Vietnam for many years. Food shortages are still a problem in some areas. Overall, 45 per cent of children in Vietnam below 5 years of age do not get enough to eat.

Following reunification in 1975 various forms of collective farming were extended to cover all Vietnam. But to stimulate production of crops, the government has issued a number of laws since 1981, gradually reintroducing private farming.

Since 1993, Vietnamese farmers can own a certificate giving them the right to farm a certain piece of land. This right can be sold and inherited. Although Vietnamese law does not strictly speaking allow the farmers to own land, in reality they can regard their land as private property. Today, collective farming has all but disappeared in the south and minority areas. However, many farmers now work together on a voluntary basis to help each other.

Pressure on farmland is high. Vietnam is so mountainous that only 21 per cent of the land can be cultivated. The two fertile deltas are the most important farming areas. They account for only 17 per cent of the land, but up to 56 per cent of Vietnam's total food production.

Agricultural machinery is seldom seen in Vietnam. This field is being irrigated using a lacquered basket on ropes and plain hard work.

MAIN CROPS, 1998 ('000 TONNES)	
Rice	29,146
Sugarcane	13,844
Vegetables	4,911
Coconut	1,106
Source: *IMF: Vietnam, 2000*	

RICE

In prehistoric times, Vietnamese culture was built up around rice farming. Today rice is still the single most important element in the Vietnamese economy. The Mekong Delta is the largest rice-growing area, with more than 90 per cent of land being used for this crop. But even the densely populated Red River Delta area produces a surplus of rice. On average, each field produces 1.8 crops per year.

Rice accounts for almost 80 per cent of the total food production in Vietnam. The industry employs people and provides the basic food of the population – eaten boiled, fried, as noodles or as rice paper wrapped around spring rolls. In hard times rice also provides the last stand against starvation. When money runs out, meat and fish are the first foods to disappear from the Vietnamese diet. Then vegetables and fruit are cut out, and finally you are left with rice. If families cannot afford all the rice they need, they will make a watery soup from it. This doesn't provide much nutrition, but at least it fools the stomach for a while.

Rice grains being sifted out from the rest of the crop. The men in the background are threshing the rice using a pedal-operated machine.

Fresh greens – including aquatic plants – are always eaten with a Vietnamese meal. These are being sold in Hoi An market.

Above Fruit and vegetables being taken to a floating market in the Mekong Delta.

Although rice is the most important crop in Vietnam, a large number of other foods are grown. Many kinds of vegetable, and fruit such as pineapple, mango, rambutan, jackfruit and orange, are grown. A large part of the tea, coffee, rubber, soy bean and peanut crop is exported. Highland areas that are not well suited for rice growing are increasingly used for these other crops.

Vietnamese products are in a difficult position on the world market. Often the quality of the manufacturing, goods, and packaging do not match world standards. Foreign businessmen sometimes complain that it is difficult for the Vietnamese to understand why the peanuts should be any better just because you put them in small plastic bags.

Left Chicken is a luxury in Vietnam. The price of one chicken is about 1–2 days full pay for an average person.

Outdated production methods and machinery make it necessary to use 20 tonnes of sugar-cane to produce one tonne of sugar in Vietnam, whereas 12–13 tonnes of sugar-cane would do in most other places. This makes it difficult for Vietnamese farmers to earn money, and consequently it is difficult for them to afford new machinery. Often Vietnamese products only earn two-thirds of the price of similar products from other countries.

Domestic animals are important both for food and for work in the fields. Although all kinds of domestic animals are found throughout the country, water buffaloes and pigs are most numerous in the north. Among minority groups buffalo-sacrificing ceremonies used to be an important part of the culture. Oxen are mostly found in central Vietnam.

1000 Dongs per agricultural worker

- 1198
- 1031-1079
- 793-846
- 675-756
- 538-603
- 413-500
- 262-392

This map shows the value of agricultural production per agricultural worker in Vietnam, by region. Some workers are able to have a much higher standard of living than workers in other regions.

DIKES

3,000 km of river dikes provide protection against floods in the Red River and Song Ma Delta areas. Destruction caused by typhoons is reduced by 2,000 km of coastal dikes which stretch from the north to central Vietnam.

N

| 0 | 100 | 200 | 300 km |

| 0 | 100 | 200 miles |

FISHING

Fish has always been an important source of protein in the Vietnamese diet. With the long coastline, the many rivers and canals and even the possibility of fishing in the paddy fields fish is easily available to most people.

Industrial fishing in the seas around Vietnam is growing in importance. Vietnam is trying to build up an export industry selling frozen or canned fish to markets like Japan, Hong Kong and Taiwan. Industrial fishing mostly takes place along the southern coast.

The early-morning fish market at Danang. It is mainly a wholesale market. Later on in the morning, retailers will take the fish to markets and restaurants around the city.

FISH SAUCE

Fish sauce is to the Vietnamese what soy sauce is to the Chinese – the universal spice or flavouring that you just cannot live without. It is made by fermenting small fish in salt and water for about nine months. The liquid is then mixed with more water, sugar, lime, chilli and garlic. It is used as a sauce for dipping spring rolls, pieces of chicken, meat or fish in. It is also added directly to meals as they are cooked.

However, industrial development means that pollution in Vietnam's waters is increasing. In some places contamination of water is more than ten times higher than WHO (World Health Organization) standards allow. In 1995 two ships collided near Ho Chi Minh City, and produced oil spills that killed many tonnes of fish, crabs, shrimps and ducks. Suddenly, 1,500 households were left without an income, and as there is no such thing as unemployment support in Vietnam, they were left on the brink of starvation.

Fishing in a canal in the Red River Delta. Fish is an easily available food for most Vietnamese.

Overfishing is another problem. In some places, the use of small-eye nets, which catch very young fish, and explosives is destroying breeding grounds and leading to depletion of fish stocks.

Below *A young boy in a circular basket boat takes fuel out to the fishing boats at Long Hai.*

Doi Moi –
Vietnamese Perestroika

Vietnam's Communist Party sees itself as a guarantee against the chaos that followed the downfall of communism in Russia. Therefore, it intends to stay in power. At the same time, the party has realized that economic development in Vietnam is urgently needed. The majority of the population works in agriculture, but because most farms only grow rice, many of these people are unemployed for half the year during the growing seasons. A large number of the unemployed are young, between 16–25 years. The government is running projects to help people start small businesses. This is an important development for the 38 million who were unemployed in 1998.

But the most important way of developing Vietnam is the policy of Doi Moi. This, like the Russian Perestroika, is changing the communist-planned economy into a free market. Doi Moi is about making money. It is a go-ahead for the Vietnamese to start private businesses, and for foreigners to invest money in the country. There are still rules, regulations and red tape, but Vietnam has moved a long way towards a free market.

The CD market in Ho Chi Minh City. The very presence of such a market illustrates that Doi Moi is working. People now have the money to buy luxuries like CDs.

Vietnam is situated in the part of the world that has the greatest economic growth – countries like China, Singapore and Thailand are developing fast. Vietnam wants to join in and leave its past behind.

The job Doi Moi has to do is a daunting one. Vietnam is one of the world's poorest countries. It still suffers from the effects of the economic embargo and decades of war. Unemployment and under-employment add to the poverty problems. Many state-owned businesses have been kept afloat by money from the government. Now they are being forced to operate in the 'survival-of-the-fittest' environment of the free market. Many have had to close down, creating more unemployment, but competitive industries are seen as essential in the long run. The aim of Doi Moi is to develop industry, transport and tourism, and eventually take Vietnam into a brighter and better future.

COMPARISON OF GROSS DOMESTIC PRODUCT (GDP) PER CAPITA AND GROWTH RATES

	GDP per capita (in US dollars)	Economic growth rate
Japan	32,350	1.1%
USA	29,240	1.8%
Germany	26,570	0.7%
United Kingdom	21,410	1.6%
Australia	20,640	2.7%
Singapore	30,170	6.0%
South Korea	8,600	4.1%
Malaysia	3,670	3.8%
Thailand	2160	3.4%
China	750	9.2%
Vietnam	350	6.1%

Source: *United Nations Human Development Report, 2000*

Even compared to other East and Southeast Asian countries Vietnam is poor. For instance, compare Vietnam's GDP with that of Malaysia. But Vietnam has now matched the spectacular growth rates of the important economies in the region – which are far higher than growth rates in the modern industrial world.

INDUSTRY

Industry only employs 12.1 per cent of the work-force in Vietnam, but produces 34.5 per cent of the Gross Domestic Product. In the future both of these figures will grow. Vietnam now wants to sell products rather than raw materials on the world market.

Traditionally, the north has placed greater emphasis on heavy industry, like other socialist countries. This is not just for ideological reasons, but also because most raw materials

Doi Moi in Vinh City

Vinh is the capital of the Nghe An province – one of the poorest in Vietnam. A 1991 guide book described Vinh as, 'very poor', and Vinh's market as, 'noteworthy for the limited selection of goods offered for sale'. Today the situation has changed. In 1990 a textile factory called 'Ho Chi Minh's Mother' built using international and government help, and also local

funds. It now employs 1,100 people and exports its products to several countries including France, Germany and Japan. A local seafood company exports frozen fish to Japan, Hong Kong and Taiwan.

The Nghe An Brewery was started in 1985 as a state-owned business. Today it has to survive on the free market. In order to do so it has imported new equipment to produce

Vinh's seafood company, successfully exporting goods to Japan, Hong Kong and Taiwan.

are found in Vietnam's Northern Mountains. The south has more light industry, such as food processing. The present policy is to encourage light industries, which produce specialized goods for particular markets.

Many Vietnamese industries are trying hard to find partners abroad, which can be difficult, especially if the business is not close to Hanoi or Ho Chi Minh City. They hope to export their products or start joint ventures with foreign companies.

high-quality beer which is able to compete with foreign brands. Sales have gone up – good for the company, but also an indicator of increased spending power in the local population. At the moment, production can't keep up with local demand, but even so exports to Sweden are being discussed.

Vinh's industries create employment and keep money flowing into this poor region of Vietnam. Today, new buildings are seen everywhere. A new airport is under construction, and Vinh's once-empty market is filled with all kinds of goods. Vinh is still not in the mainstream of developments, but Doi Moi has changed the lives of a lot of people there.

Above *The production line at Hghe An brewery.*

Right *The dyeing hall at the textile factory in Vinh.*

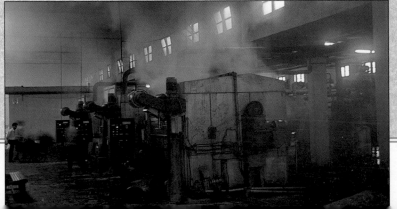

TRANSPORT

Travelling in Vietnam is usually a slow and overcrowded experience. Roads, bridges and railways were prime targets during the wars. Reconstruction has been slow, and lack of maintenance since 1975 has not improved the situation. The poor infrastructure prevents economic growth spreading from the big centres in Hanoi

A ferry on the river at Hoi An. Nothing is wasted in Vietnam – least of all space on public transport.

and Ho Chi Minh City. The building and improvement of roads, railways and airports will therefore play a significant role in the development of the country.

The need for an efficient transportation system to tie the country together is relatively new. Formerly, the northern and southern parts of Vietnam had little to do with each other economically. In addition, the Vietnamese as a nation do not travel a lot, so the need for efficient means of transport down through the country was not pressing.

Only 15 per cent of Vietnam's roads are covered by an asphalt surface. And even those are often in poor condition. National Highway One – the road linking Hanoi and Ho Chi Minh City – is not the major motorway it would be in an industrialized country. In some places the traffic is a mixture of water buffaloes, mopeds, bicycles, heavy trucks, slow, overloaded buses, a few fast modern cars and the occasional dog. A truck seldom manages more than 35 km per hour.

'We are preparing the equipment for building the new highway between Hanoi and Ho Chi Minh City. Better transport is very important. It will help us develop Vinh City and the villages of the Nghe An province faster.' – **Ho Xuan Hung, Chairman of the People Committee of the Nghe An Province**

36

Express trains between Hanoi and Ho Chi Minh City run at an average speed of 40 km per hour – about the same speed as the French trains that ran in 1936. The central government has approved an ambitious plan to reconstruct the tracks, 319 stations, 1,533 bridges and 39 tunnels. By the year 2020 genuine high-speed trains should link the major cities. New lines are planned, whilst those that are used infrequently will close.

This is National Highway One, running between Hanoi and Ho Chi Minh City. The road is used for drying rice grains, as well as for driving.

In the past, Vietnam Airlines was notorious for its ancient aeroplanes. The fleet is now being modernized and greatly expanded. New domestic and international routes are being added to the route network, and the number of passengers is growing steadily. Doi Moi in the air means that today new companies are starting up to compete with Vietnam Airlines.

THE MOTORBIKES OF HO CHI MINH CITY

Few Vietnamese can afford a car, but more and more can afford a motorbike, especially in Ho Chi Minh City. Here, the number of motorbikes on the road will soon reach one million. These vehicles now account for daily traffic jams and 60 per cent of serious air pollution in the city. Many riders cover their faces as protection against the dust and fumes.

FOREIGN INVESTMENT

It was a day of celebration in Vietnam when President Clinton lifted the US embargo in 1994. Even so, other countries had already started doing business with Vietnam. The Chinese minority had played an important role in the economy of South Vietnam before 1975. Later, many of them left the country, but others stayed. As a result, many Vietnamese Chinese had relatives in other countries. These people were among the first to take advantage of Doi Moi, and it is no coincidence that countries like Taiwan, Hong Kong and Singapore top the list of Vietnam's foreign investors.

Western companies have also moved into Vietnam to sell their products and open up factories, bringing some foreign workers with them. New houses are being built to accommodate these people and their families. Both housing and office space are in short supply in Vietnam's cities. As a result, office prices in Hanoi are now on the same level as prices in London, and above those in New York City.

Generally speaking, the Vietnamese want to work for foreign companies, as salaries can be much higher than the Vietnamese average. On the other hand, some foreign companies are reputed to treat their staff very badly. Working conditions can be appalling, and some workers complain of beatings and sexual harassment. But the driving force for most Vietnamese is to earn money for the family, so many just put up with this treatment.

Foreign investment is far from evenly spread around the country. Ho Chi Minh City attracts about half of it – which is three times more than Hanoi. Hanoi, however, has attracted 255 times as much investment as the poorer Nghe An province.

FOREIGN INVESTORS IN VIETNAM, 1998	
Country	Total Capital invested (US dollars in millions)
Taiwan	194
Hong Kong	105
Singapore	224
South Korea	200
Japan	541
Australia	6
Malaysia	111
France	74
USA	11

Source: *IMF, 2000*

Selling toys

Buying a toy is something new in Vietnam, and a good indicator of the rising standard of living. Tran Toung Nhi had to make her own toys from whatever she could find when she was growing up in Ho Chi Minh City. Today, she is a product manager selling toys made by the multinational company, Lego, from special shops at Western prices. These toys are extremely expensive for the average Vietnamese person, but even so most customers are Vietnamese. Lego is the first high-quality toy to be sold in Vietnam. Apart from being new and exciting, the toys are bought for their educational value.

Tran Toung Nhi is not married. Therefore, like other working relatives, she gives all her salary to her mother.

'Some customers are rich, but others are just ordinary people who have saved money to buy a small box. One such man rode his bicycle 30 km from Bien Hoa to buy one for his son. People here like to do much for their children.' – **Tran Toung Nhi, Ho Chi Minh City**

Battlefield tourism at the Cu Chi tunnels outside Ho Chi Minh City, where Vietnamese guerrillas once hid. The guide explains how the tunnels were made narrow, so the larger Americans had difficulty moving inside them.

NUMBER OF TOURISTS	
1992	400,000
1994	1,000,000
1997	1,700,000

INCOME FROM TOURISM	
Income from hotels and restaurants (billions of dongs)	
1993	5,119
1994	6,125
1995	8,625
1996	9,776
1997	11,307
1999	12,404

TOURISM

The Vietnamese government has high expectations of the tourism industry, and hopes for 4 million tourists annually by the year 2000. Tourists spend money, and money is just what Vietnam needs. Vietnam has lots to offer – beautiful scenery, beaches and interesting historical and cultural sites. Old battlefields are attracting increasing numbers of visitors. Some are former American soldiers who return to visit the places where they once fought.

Foreign visitors are usually well received by the Vietnamese, who are eager to make contact with the outside world. After years of war, isolation and poverty, many simply want to meet people from other countries. Others want to practise their English, since job advertisements for foreign companies usually include a demand for 'excellent English'. Other Vietnamese are eager to make as much money as possible by selling souvenirs or providing services. Generally speaking, contact with tourists offers a far better income than work as a teacher, policeman or doctor. An English-speaking tourist guide can easily earn a teacher's weekly wage in a single day.

The area around the famous hotels of downtown Ho Chi Minh City is a favourite haunt for young Vietnamese who want to practise their English on foreigners.

Doi Moi at the Perfume Pagoda

One religious site that has seen a revival in recent years is the Perfume Pagoda, south of Hanoi. The Perfume Pagoda is actually a number of pagodas, shrines and caves tucked away along a mountain path. In the biggest cave an incarnation of Buddha is said to have transformed into the female Goddess of Mercy. Between March and April pilgrims travel there in small boats by the thousands. Pilgrims have made this journey for hundreds of years, but since the advent of Doi Moi, travellers are offered all kinds of food, souvenirs and services by enterprising salespeople. You can even walk straight from one pagoda into a karaoke bar. The Vietnamese do not see a problem in this – piety and enjoyment do not have to oppose each other. As this period is the rice-growing season, unemployed people come here to beg. Some beggars have fully understood the spirit of the new times, and have invested in microphones or loudspeakers to raise their voices above all competition on their patch of mountain path.

Even electric guitars are used to try to earn a little money by musicians on the path to the Perfume Pagoda.

A poor country?

Vietnam is indeed a poor country when measured using economic criteria. With a GDP of only US$ 350 per head, Vietnam is placed as number 108 out of 174 countries in the world. However, Vietnam moves forward if it is measured using other criteria, such as literacy rates and life expectancy. Brazil's GDP per head is over 13 times higher than Vietnam's, but life expectancy is almost 1 year lower. China has more than double Vietnam's GDP, but only an 82.8 per cent literacy rate compared to Vietnam's 92.9 per cent. Thanks to the fact that Vietnam is rich in human resources, it has been able to make good use of its limited economic resources. Of course, Vietnam does have problems. For example, half of the population has no access to clean drinking water, and two million people have no access to health services.

Only 55 per cent of children attend secondary school.

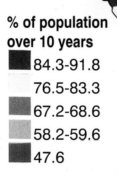

0 100 200 300 km

0   100   200 miles

N

% of population over 10 years

- 84.3-91.8
- 76.5-83.3
- 67.2-68.6
- 58.2-59.6
- 47.6

Right *Map showing the percentage of population over 10 years of age that can read, in different regions of Vietnam.*

EDUCATION

Vietnam has a far better-developed health and education system than might be expected from its level of economic development. In the cities around 99 per cent of all children attend a primary school, although the percentage is lower in the countryside. Children go to school six days a week and often have private lessons on Sundays in the teacher's home.

One of Doi Moi's aims has been to reduce public spending. Funds for the social sectors have been cut, affecting both health and education. Today slightly fewer children attend school than 20 years ago. Some teachers complain that students are less willing to study hard, because it's so easy to make money from the tourists instead.

HEALTH

Most doctors in Vietnam practise Western medicine, but one in seven practise traditional Chinese/Vietnamese medicine. The state of the health sector is one of the most important differences between an industrialized country and a developing one. Malnutrition, poverty, low levels of development and difficult climatic conditions in Vietnam mean that people are more likely to suffer from serious diseases than people in the West. The Vietnamese also have to pay for medicine, even though many cannot afford it. In the past, treatment from the health service was free. Now, all but the extremely poor have to pay for hospital treatment. The health sector does receive foreign aid, but much improvement is still needed.

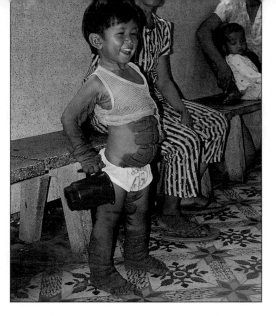

Above *This child has elephantitis, a disease caused by a parasite which can grow to a length of 5 cm. The disease is passed on by mosquitoes.*

Left *In the past, people had to travel to the health care station by ox cart – a slow and uncomfortable experience. Foreign aid has helped to fund more efficient means of transport, such as this three-wheeled ambulance.*

QUALITY OF LIFE (1998)		
	Vietnam	**Developing world average**
Life expectancy	67.4 years	64.4 years
Adult literacy rate	92.9%	72.7%
Under-5 infant mortality rate	42 deaths/1,000 born	93 deaths/1,000 born
One-year olds immunized against tuberculosis	98%	82%
Percentage of adults aged 15–49 living with HIV/AIDS	0.22%	1.18%

Source: *UNDP Human Development Report, 2000*

The happy ending?

The improvement in the standard of living in the countryside is shown by the rising number of brick houses. So boats transporting bricks, like this one in the Red River Delta, are a sign of hope for the future.

Unfortunately, there is no guarantee that happy times are just around the corner for everyone in Vietnam.

Doi Moi is certainly working, and Vietnam will experience great economic growth over the next few years. But it remains to be seen if it will spread to all parts of the country. Some people are becoming very rich in Vietnam. Others are raising their standard of living to the level of people in countries like Thailand, but many have not yet seen much improvement in their life-style.

Further military conflict in the future cannot be ruled out. All the countries around the South China Sea (including Vietnam) claim ownership of the Paracel and Spratly islands. There may be oil under these islands, and countries are attempting to prove their historical right to them. Many countries, especially China, are building up their naval power, in order to defend the islands if they occupy them.

44

This man has his own balloon-selling business – a colourful reminder of the growth of free enterprise in Vietnam.

Will the presence of foreign companies in Vietnam be a blessing in the long run? Or will they just generate income for themselves, using Vietnam's cheap labour? Some foreign companies are beginning to cut the already-low wages for workers, and strikes have occurred. Pollution, prostitution and lack of money to pay for education and health-care are other problems the Vietnamese will have to deal with in the future.

Vietnam is a remarkable nation by any standards. Other countries have received huge amounts of aid and have remained poor. Vietnam has been bombed, devastated by war and left to stand on its own. It has still managed to move on. Given its history, Vietnam today could not be anything but poor. But the Vietnamese are very resourceful people. In the past they have surprised the world by winning wars against all odds. In the future they might surprise the world once more by winning the peace, too.

'I'm only 20 but Vietnam has changed a lot in my lifetime. We used to say that a house, a wife and a buffalo were the most important things in a man's life. Now it's a house, wife and motorbike. We have more opportunities now. I hope to make a career in international banking.'
– Linh, aged 20, Hanoi

Glossary

Boat people Refugees who left Vietnam by boat.

Caodaism A Vietnamese religion that combines elements of Vietnamese and Chinese religions with Islam, Christianity, Hinduism and a belief in the spirit world.

Collective farming An operation where several farmers work together on the same land, and are paid in the same way as if they worked in a factory.

Communism The political idea that everything should be owned and controlled by the community for its own benefit, instead of being for the benefit of a few rich people.

Defoliant A chemical that removes leaves from trees and plants. Commonly used by the military in order to see clearly through forests.

Delta A triangular area of land found at the mouth of a river enclosed by surrounding streams, and usually rich in minerals.

Dike A long, low wall built to avoid flooding around coasts and rivers.

Doi Moi A Vietnamese economic policy, introduced in 1986, that aims to transform the economy and modernize the country.

Gross Domestic Product (GDP) The value of all goods and services produced in a country during one year.

Infrastructure The infrastructure of a country is made up of the things that help it to function well: roads, railways, airports, ports and schools, for example.

Indochinese Union A former French colony made up of what are now Vietnam, Cambodia and Laos.

Liberated Set free, or released, from enemy occupation and allowed to become an individual country again.

Lunar new year festival The old Vietnamese calendar follows the moon, so traditional Vietnamese New Year falls between 21 January and 20 February in the Western calendar.

Malnutrution A lack of sufficient nutrients, usually due to a lack of food.

Mediums People who say they can contact spirits.

Monopolies The right to be the only person or company that can buy or sell a particular kind of product.

Paddy fields Fields where rice is grown.

Pagoda A Buddist sacred building, found all over Vietnam.

Perestroika A Russian word used to describe the removal of government controls from industries.

Piety The ability to follow the commands and teachings of a particular religion.

Second World War This war was fought in Europe and the Pacific from 1939–1945. The Allies (the USA, the Soviet Union, Britain, France, Australia, New Zealand and Canada amongst others) defeated the Axis powers (Germany, Italy, Japan and others).

Further information

Asia Observer – Vietnam
Website: www.asiaobserver.com/vietnam.htm
News and background information on Vietnam.

ActionAid
Hamlyn House, Archway, London N19 5PG
Tel: 020 7561 7561   Website: www.actionaid.org
ActionAid works in Vietnam on farming, health and water projects.

Department for International Development
94 Victoria St, London SW1E 5JL
Website: www.dfid.gov.uk
General information on developing countries.

Investigating the Vietnam War
Website: www.spartacus.schoolnet.co.uk/vietnam.html
A website for schools with excellent material.

Lonely Planet – Destination Vietnam
Website: www.lonelyplanet.com/dest/sea/vietnam.htm

Oxfam
274 Banbury Rd, Oxford OX2 7DZ
Website: www.oxfam.org.uk/coolplanet
Good web pages on Vietnam.

UNICEF, 55 Lincoln's Inn Fields, London WC2A 3NB
Website: www.unicef.org.uk
Resources for schools about people in other lands.

Books to read

A Family from Vietnam by Simon Scoones (Hodder Wayland, 1998)

World Focus: Vietnam by Pat Simmons (Heinemann, 1995)

You can also find out about Vietnam from travel guide books, such as the *Lonely Planet* and the *Rough Guide to Vietnam*.

Index

Numbers in **bold** refer to illustrations.